NEW Chatterbox

2

Pupil's Book

Derek Strange

OXFORD
UNIVERSITY PRESS

Hello again!

01 Listen and read.

Hi, Poppy! Hi, Bean!

Hi, Woody.

How are you?

I'm fine, thanks.

Don't forget your bag, Woody!

Don't go too slowly, Poppy!

No ... where's the accelerator?

02 Listen again and point to the right picture.

Ask and answer.

Where are the three friends?

They're at the funfair.

Who has got a bike?

Don't ... Where ...?

AT THE FUNFAIR

The fox and the box

(04) Listen and repeat.

The fox is near the box.
The bear is on the chair.
The snake is under the
    pencil case.
The parrot is in the air!

Ask and answer. Where are the foxes now?

Read and match.

1 The red fox is …   on a tall giraffe.

2 The blue fox is …   near a fat hippo.

3 The yellow fox is …   under a hungry lion.

4 The green fox is …   in a safari car.

5 The white fox is …   on the happy elephant.

in, on, near, under

Where are the bears?

 Listen and sing.

> Where is the happy hippopotamus?
>
> Where are the dancing bears?
>
> Where, where is the big grey elephant?
>
> Is she here? Is she there?
>
> There is the happy hippopotamus!
>
> There are the dancing bears!
>
> There is the big grey elephant!
>
> She's there, she's there, she's there!

Read and choose an answer.

1. Where are Ken, Kate and their friends? — Grey.
2. Where is the elephant? → Under the tree.
3. What colour is the elephant? In a box.
4. Where are the bears? Near a car.
5. Where is the hippo? In the tree-house.

From thirteen to twenty

🎧 **Listen, repeat and clap your hands.**

thirteen **13**   fourteen **14**   fifteen **15**   sixteen **16**   seventeen **17**   eighteen **18**   nineteen **19**   twenty **20**

⚪ **Look at the pictures. Find seven differences.**

⚪ **Answer the questions.**

Picture a

1. How many crayons are there?
2. How many notebooks are there?
3. How many balls are there?

Picture b

4. How many *New Chatterbox* books are there?
5. How many pencils are there?
6. How many letters of the ABC are there?

🎧 **Now listen and answer Yes or No.**

MORE ABOUT DOCTOR ROTTER

1 How many golden cockatoos are there in the world? Only one? Ha! Ha!

Don't talk about the golden cockatoo here, Rotter – not near a policeman!

2 'The golden cockatoo' – what's that?

Maybe it's the name of a restaurant?

Let's ask Luke – he can tell us.

3 Hi, Bean. I'm in New York with Captain Shadow ... we're at a meeting of international detectives.

Wow! ... Can you help us, Luke? Who is Doctor Rotter? And what's 'the golden cockatoo'?

4 Wait a second ... Here's something: 'The Golden Cockatoo is a very rare bird, from Australia' ... Oh, good! Captain Shadow is here – she can tell you about Doctor Rotter ...

5 Doctor Rotter? Yes, I know him. He's a famous con-man. The police are always interested in the Doctor ...

6 But why is Doctor Rotter in London? ... To get that packet?

Perhaps it's for his 'golden cockatoo' plan?

Mmm, maybe. ... Can you watch the Doctor for me, Bean? Call me tomorrow.

OK, Captain!

Number 32, School Street

09 **Listen and repeat.**

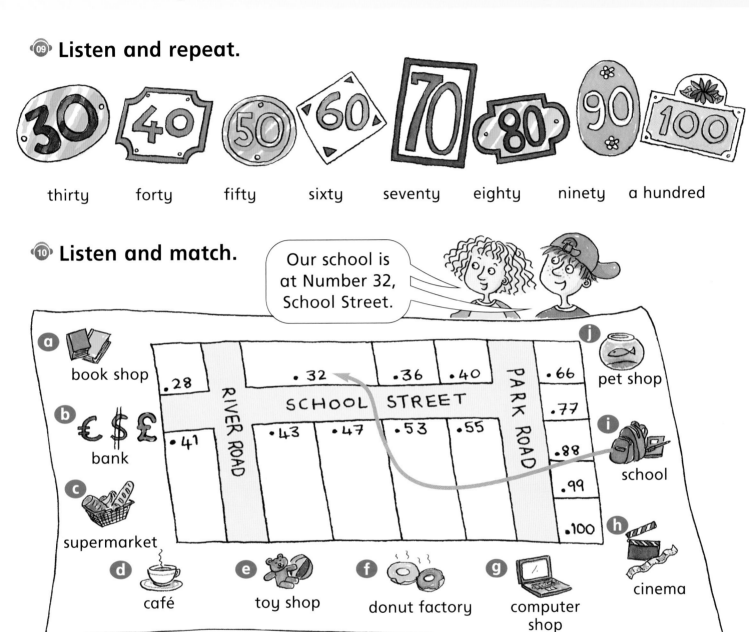

thirty   forty   fifty   sixty   seventy   eighty   ninety   a hundred

10 **Listen and match.**

Look at the map. Ask and answer.

Crazy counting

 **Listen and repeat.**

Six and six is sixty-six
Three and O is thirty
Eight and eight is eighty-eight
Ten and O's a hundred!

> Count some more!

Nine and nine is ninety-nine
Five and O is fifty
Seven and seven is seventy-seven
Ten and O's a hundred!

> Count again!

Four and four is forty-four
Two and O is twenty
One and seven is seventeen
Ten and O's a hundred!

 Play Bingo.

> Forty!
> Eighty! ...

1 Game 1. Choose and write down five of these numbers:
  10 – 20 – 30 – 40 – 50 – 60 – 70 – 80 – 90 – 100.

2 Play Bingo with your friends.

3 Game 2. Choose five numbers from 10 to 20.
  Play Bingo! with them.

4 Game 3. Choose five numbers from 30 to 50.
  Play Bingo! with them.

Lucy at the sweet shop

(12) Listen and point.

… And can I have two fresh worms for Herman and Shep, please?

Two fresh worms – here you are!

● **Listen again and write numbers in five boxes.**

two donuts

six chocolate elephants

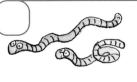

two fresh worms

four tomato lollipops

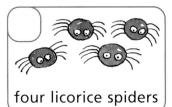

four licorice spiders

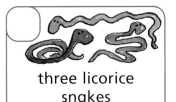

three licorice snakes

five chocolate chip cookies

three peppermint dinosaurs

● **Ask and answer.**

Have you got my tomato lollipops?

No, I haven't.

Have you got our fresh worms?

Yes, I have. I've got two fresh worms for you!

Can I have …? + plural nouns

SECRET POWDER

10 o'clock the next morning.

Have you got the tickets for New York, Bubble?

I've got them here, Doc.

To Waterloo Station, please.

New York?

They're in a taxi, Bean ... Yes ... To Waterloo Station. Meet me there now, and bring Poppy!

Look! It's that boy! The boy at the funfair – remember?

Yeah! He was near our hotel this morning too!

Where's the packet of secret powder?

It's OK, Rotter! I've got it.

Secret powder? What's this powder?

They've got tickets for the boat to New York!

Yes, and Captain Shadow is already in New York!

TRAINS TO SOUTHAMPTON FOR THE BOAT TO NEW YORK

Let's call Luke and Captain Shadow.

Mum's shopping list

🎧 **Listen. Tick the six things on Mum's list.**

⚫ **Look at Herman's basket.
What is missing from Mum's list?**

⚫ **Play a game: Can you remember?**

Look at the pictures again for one minute. Close your books.

Work with a friend and write down the ten things in the picture. Then open your books and check: *We've got the jar of honey, but we haven't got the ...!*

a bag of / a bottle of / a box of / a can of / a packet of / a piece of ...

The Sweet Shop Song

🔊 **Listen and sing.**

I've got a great big packet of peppermints
And a great big jar of jam.
I've got a great big bottle of sunshine –
My name's 'Sweet Shop Sam'!

Sweet Shop Sam, Sweet Shop Sam –
He's our friendly Sweet Shop man!

I've got a great big piece of banana cake
And some great big worms in a can.
I've got a great big bag of spiders –
My name's 'Sweet Shop Sam'!

Sweet Shop Sam, Sweet Shop Sam –
He's our friendly Sweet Shop man!

⚫ **Look and say. What is it?**

> I love cooking! Here are two of my favourite dishes.

Read and match.

a

b

c

d

1 'Shepherd's Pie' is a popular British dish. You need meat, onions and mashed potatoes for it. It sometimes has peas and carrots in it too.

2 We have sweet dishes in Britain too. 'Apple Crumble' is my favourite. It has apples and sugar under the 'crumble'. You need flour, butter and sugar for the 'crumble'. It's delicious!

Here's my easy recipe for CRUMBLE.

1 Put 225 grams of flour into a bowl.
2 Put in 75 grams of soft butter. Mix the flour and butter together with your fingers.
3 Now put 100 grams of brown sugar into the bowl and mix it with your fingers again.
4 Put the crumble mixture on cooked apples and cook it at 180°C for 35 minutes.

Bubble's game

Take turns: throw a dice.

A You can go to the next box and answer the question only when you throw [dice] [dice] or [dice]

B You can go to the next box and answer the question only when you throw [dice] [dice] or [dice]

START HERE

1 Say this number: **18**

2 Where is London?

3 Is there a park near your school?

4 What are the missing words in this rhyme?

The fox is _____ the box.
The bear is _____ the chair.
The snake is _____ the pencil case.
The parrot is _____ the air!

5 Say the 'Crazy Counting' rap again. (page 8)

6 What's this?

30 LICORICE SPIDERS

7 How many spiders are in the packet?

8 What's the answer? **37 + 63 = ?**

9 What's your favourite dish?

10 Say this quickly:
Big Blue Bubbles ...
Big Blue Bubbles ...
Big Blue Bubbles ...
Big Blue Bubbles

FINISH

An evening at home

🎧 Listen, repeat and point.

a) Shep
b) Dad and Annie
c) Mum
d) Lucy
e) Gran and Herman
f) Gramp

● Now read and match.

He's playing the guitar.	a	He's playing with his pet spider.	
They're making cookies.		She's reading a comic.	
They're watching a video.		She's drinking a can of lemonade.	

● Who is it? Ask and answer.

She's reading a comic – who is it?

They're watching a video.

Lucy.

Annie and Dad.

She's watching = She is watching
They're watching = They are watching

NEW YORK! NEW YORK!

He's eating my ice cream

19 **Listen and number.**

● **Right or wrong? Write ✔ or ✗.**

In picture 1 the boy is eating an ice cream.

In picture 2 the girl is writing a letter.

In picture 3 they're making donuts.

In picture 4 they're playing basketball.

In picture 5 she's reading a dictionary.

In picture 6 he's opening a bottle of milk.

He's writing. He isn't reading … They're drinking. They're not eating.

In the park

(20) Listen and point.

● Who is it? Read and match.

1. It's eating the old man's donuts. `g`
2. They're riding their bikes. ☐
3. He's making a paper aeroplane. ☐
4. She's pointing at the balloons. ☐
5. He's playing a guitar. ☐
6. She's talking to a friend on her mobile. ☐
7. He's reading a book. He isn't watching the dog. ☐
8. They're playing with a toy boat. ☐

The 'Panda Bears' rap
(21) Listen and repeat.

I'm dreaming … I'm dreaming:
The panda bears are waking up –
They're dancing round my bed!
And suddenly I'm dancing too –
I'm dancing in my head.
Zzz … Zzz … Zzz.

An adventure at the beach

(22) Listen, read and repeat.

Lucy, Shep and Herman are going to the beach. They're waiting for the bus. It's coming now!

Lucy is running into the sea. She's wearing arm bands. She's got a toy whale.

A huge wave is coming in fast! Lucy is looking round and running to the beach – can she escape?

Herman and Shep are pulling Lucy out of the water – she's safe!

● Read and match.

1 Are they waiting for a bus?...
2 Are they going to school? ...
3 Is Lucy wearing a hat? ...
4 Is Lucy wearing arm bands in the sea?...
5 Is Herman swimming with Lucy?...
6 Is Shep helping his sister?...

Yes, she is.
Yes, he is.
Yes, they are.
No, she isn't.
No, he isn't.
No, they're not.

● Ask and answer.

Is the bus coming?

Are they going to school?

Yes, it is.

No, they're not.

Is she wearing ...? Yes, she is. / No, she isn't.

YANKEE STADIUM

1 Twenty minutes later.

They're going into that hotel, Pluto.

Hey! That's Doctor Rotter – he's going into the hotel! Is he staying here?

I dunno. Let's ask him ...

2 Are you staying in this hotel, Doctor?

Yes, I am. I'm staying here for three days.

Are you working in New York, Doc?

3 I'm planning an important experiment ... for my research.

We're visiting our auntie here.

Yeah, our auntie ... er ... it's her birthday ...

4 Powder ... and an important experiment ... Mmm. So what is Dr Rotter's 'research' this time? Let's watch him carefully, Pluto.

5 That evening.

We're standing across the street from their hotel, Poppy ... Wait! Doctor Rotter is coming out of the hotel! Maybe he's going to a secret meeting!

6 At the stadium.

It's a false alarm, Pluto – he's only watching a baseball game!

It's Frankie again!

(24) Listen and look at the pictures.

● Listen again. Read and match.

He's going into the shop
next to the café. ☐

He's coming across the street.
He's carrying a bag. ☐

He's getting out of the car now.
Yes – it's Frankie the Fox! [1]

He's coming out of the shop.
He's holding an ice cream –
he's going to the beach! ☐

He's walking round the car … ☐

● Ask and answer.

What's
Frankie doing
in picture 1?

He's getting out
of the white car.
What's he doing
in picture 2?

● Answer the questions.

1 Who is watching Frankie?

2 Where is she standing?

3 What is Frankie carrying?

4 Where is the ice cream shop?

5 What is Frankie doing today?

across   into   next to   out of   round

If you're feeling sad and blue ...

● **Read and choose: is or are.**

1 (Is) Are she making a pizza?

2 My brothers is are playing a new video game.

3 They is are sitting under a tree near the beach.

4 He is are eating all the donuts!

5 Is Are you going to school?

🎧 **Listen, sing and dance.**

What can you do ...
If you're feeling sad and blue?
If you're feeling all unhappy
And you don't know what to do?

Well now, listen. Here's my advice ...
You can skip out of your corner,
You can dance across the room,
You can spin round and round,
And then dance back again!

Just skip out of your corner,
Dance across the room,
Spin round and round
And dance back again!

It's raining

🎧26 Listen and repeat.

The sun is shining. It's a hot, sunny day.

The wind is blowing. It's a windy day.

It's raining. It's a wet, rainy day.

It's snowing. It's a very cold day.

⬤ Read and match.

🎧27 Listen and point.

1 It's really windy today! And cold, too.

2 Great! It's snowing again. Come on – let's get the toboggan!

3 It's hot today. Let's go to the swimming pool.

4 Oh no – it's raining. We can't play tennis now.

It's hot. It's windy.

THE COMPETITION AND THE PRIZE

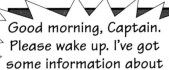

1 Good morning, Captain. Please wake up. I've got some information about the golden cockatoo!

OK, OK, Luke. What's the news?

2 Here it is, Captain. It's a message from the San Francisco Bird Club, in California …

★ ★ ★ COMPETITION ★ ★ ★
The San Francisco Bird Club is having a competition to find a Golden Cockatoo.
We are offering a prize of
$$$ ONE MILLION DOLLARS $$$
for this rare bird!
★ Can you catch and bring us a Golden Cockatoo?
Please look at our website for more information.

3 So **that's** Doctor Rotter's plan! He's hoping to win the prize! … But how? Let's find out, Pluto!

Right, Captain – good luck!

4 It's a sunny day, Rotter – let's walk to Central Park.

OK. Maybe we can find a squirrel there … have you got the powder?

A squirrel? Maybe that's for his experiment.

5 I haven't got the secret powder, Doc. It isn't here.

Don't worry, Squeak. There are no squirrels here today …

6 We can do the experiment tomorrow, on Liberty Island. There are squirrels on Liberty Island!

That's a cool plan, Doc. Then we can go back to San Francisco for the real business!

Yeah. You can do your job at the Zoo for us, Bubble …

The World Weather rap

(29) Listen and repeat.

In Antarctica it's snowing
And in Mexico it's hot.
In Japan the wind is blowing,
And in Italy it's not.
In Brazil the sun is shining,
And in Spain the sky is blue.
In Turkey now it's raining,
And in Greece it's rainy too.

● Read and match.

1 Where is it sunny today?	In Antarctica.
2 Where is it windy?	In Japan.
3 Where is it wet and rainy?	In Brazil and Spain.
4 Where is it a cold day?	In Mexico.
5 Where is it a very hot day?	In Greece and Turkey.

● Ask and answer.

Is it raining today in Japan?

Is it sunny in Spain today?

No, it isn't.

Yes, it is.

Is it raining in Spain today?

A holiday postcard

● **Read and match. Choose: A or B?**

● **Answer the questions.**

1. Who is writing this postcard?
2. Who is she writing to?
3. Where is her family's hotel?
4. Where is she sitting?
5. What is today's weather in Spain?
6. What is her sister doing?

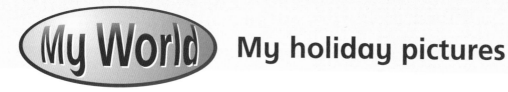

My World — My holiday pictures

● Read and match.

Here are some of my holiday photos – come and have a look.

☐ In this photo, I'm on a boat on the River Thames, near London. That's in the south of England. The Thames is a beautiful river.

☐ This is a photo of a holiday with my aunt and my cousins in Scotland. We're on a mountain in this picture – there are some great mountains and lakes in Scotland. Edinburgh is a nice city, too.

☐ This is a picture of me, in Wales last year, at a mountain bike centre. There are some good bike trails in the Black Mountains of Wales.

● Match the photos with the places on the map. Write: A, B or C.

☐ Scotland
☐ England
☐ Wales

● Quiz about Britain.

1 What is the capital city of England?

2 What is the capital city of Scotland?

3 What is the name of the big river in London?

The Question Cookies Game

Take turns: throw a dice.

A You can go to the next box and answer the question only when you throw or

B You can go to the next box and answer the question only when you throw or

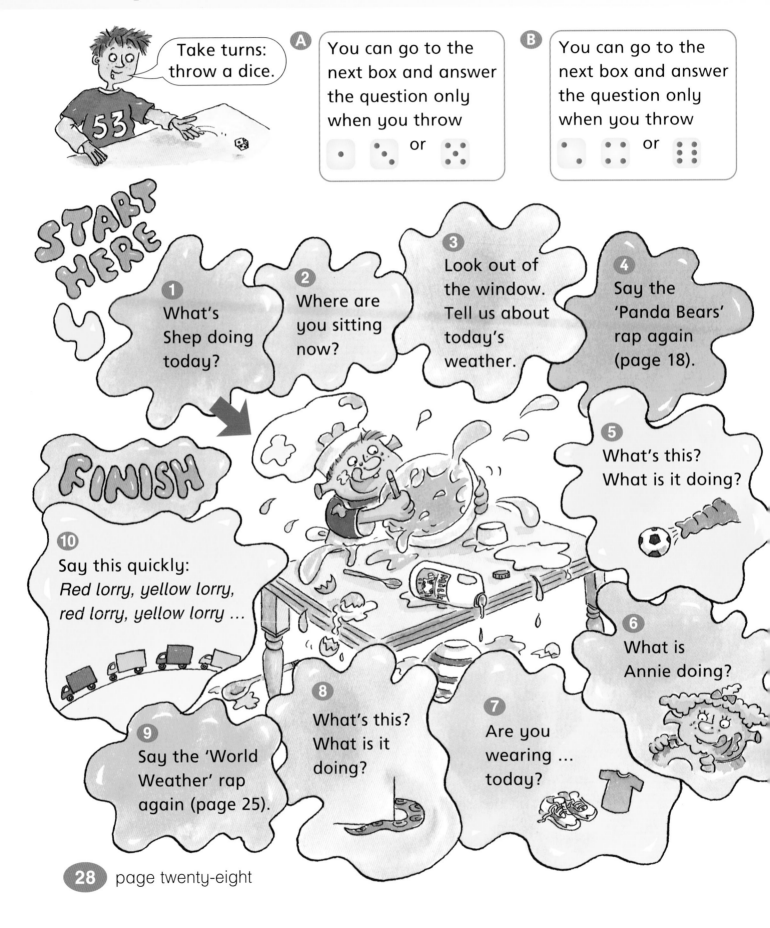

START HERE

1 What's Shep doing today?

2 Where are you sitting now?

3 Look out of the window. Tell us about today's weather.

4 Say the 'Panda Bears' rap again (page 18).

5 What's this? What is it doing?

FINISH

10 Say this quickly: *Red lorry, yellow lorry, red lorry, yellow lorry ...*

9 Say the 'World Weather' rap again (page 25).

8 What's this? What is it doing?

7 Are you wearing ... today?

6 What is Annie doing?

I like pop music

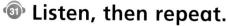 **Listen, then repeat.**

Welcome to Melody McSong! Melody, what's your favourite music?

Well, I like pop music. I like classical music, too.

And what's your favourite relaxation – computer games?

Oh no! I don't like computer games ... I don't like computers!

Listen and choose: like **or** don't like.

1 I like (don't like) ghost films.
2 I like don't like books.
3 I like don't like football on TV.
4 I like don't like dance music.
5 I like don't like adventure films.
6 I like don't like news programmes on TV.

I like ... I don't like ...

ON THE FERRY

The next morning.

... they're planning to do their experiment today, on Liberty Island, and then go back to California tomorrow. I'm planning to follow them ...

That's really lucky, Captain! Bean and I have got ten days' holiday in San Francisco, from tomorrow ... with our cousin, Peggy-Sue! So we can all help you!

That's fantastic! We can beat Dr Rotter now! See you in San Francisco!

Cookies, cookies
I like cookies
I like cookies
Every day ...
Ha! Ha! Ha!

LIBERTY

Do **you** like cookies, bird? Here's a special cookie for you ... a **very** 'special' cookie. Ha! Ha!

What's his game now? Is his 'special cookie' part of the experiment? ... Watch that cookie carefully, Pluto.

Do you like sports?

34 **Listen and repeat.**

● **Ask and answer:** Yes, I do. **or** No, I don't.

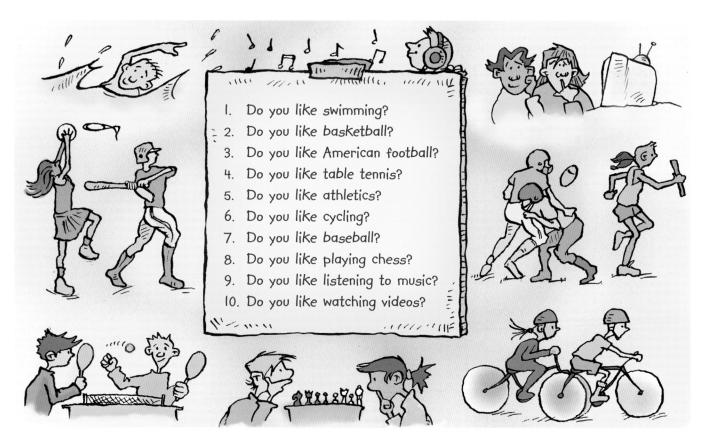

I. Do you like swimming?
2. Do you like basketball?
3. Do you like American football?
4. Do you like table tennis?
5. Do you like athletics?
6. Do you like cycling?
7. Do you like baseball?
8. Do you like playing chess?
9. Do you like listening to music?
10. Do you like watching videos?

● **Write true answers to the questions.**

I don't like swimming. ... I like basketball.

Do you like ...? Yes, I do. / No, I don't. page thirty-one **31**

I don't like the rain!

🎧 **Listen and sing.** 🎵

I like the sun in summer,
But I don't like the rain!
I like the snow in winter,
But I don't like the rain!
Say it again: I don't like the rain!
No, no, no, no: I don't like the rain!

I like the wind in autumn,
But I don't like the rain!
I like the flowers in springtime,
But I don't like the rain!
Say it again: I don't like the rain!
No, no, no, no: I don't like the rain!

⬤ **Write true answers:** Yes, I do. **or** No, I don't.

① Do you like classical music?
② Do you like comics?
③ Do you like story books?

④ Do you like cooking?
⑤ Do you like rainy days at home?

Interesting animals

Listen, read and point.

Its name: cockatoo
Its countries: Australia, Malaysia and the Philippines
Its colour: white. (Sometimes yellow, pink or black)
Its food: seeds, nuts, worms from trees

Its name: snow leopard
Its countries: India and Pakistan (The Himalayas)
Its colours: grey, white and black
Its food: rabbits, other small animals, fish

Its name: porcupine
Its countries: Kenya (and other countries of Africa)
Its colours: grey, black and white
Its food: fruit, roots, worms and other insects

Its name: 'Komodo Dragon'
Its country: The Komodo Islands of Indonesia
Its colours: grey and brown
Its food: small animals, and (sometimes) people

Read and match.

1 It's a very big lizard, and has a long tail. It eats small animals ... and sometimes it eats people!

2 It eats nuts, seeds, and worms. It's white.

3 It's big. It's grey, black and white. It eats rabbits, fish and other small animals.

4 It eats worms and roots. It sometimes eats insects, too.

Play a game.

Think of an animal ...

It eats leaves. ... Sometimes it's grey, sometimes it's white, and sometimes it's brown ...

It's an elephant!

No. It's not very big. It eats carrots, too.

It eats ...

PLUTO AND THE COOKIE

He doesn't like lemonade!

(38) Listen and repeat.

Pluto likes cookies ...

... but he doesn't like lemonade.

**(39) Look. What do Caroline's pets like?
Listen and point to the right pet.**

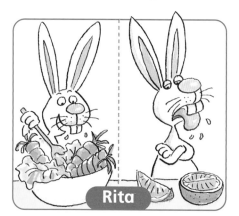

Rita

Tom

SEEDS   Bob

⬤ Right or wrong? Write ✔ or ✗.

❶ Tom likes milk. ☐

❷ He likes fish. ☐

❸ Rita likes carrots and leaves. ☐

❹ She doesn't like oranges. ☐

❺ Bob doesn't like nuts and seeds. ☐

❻ He likes worms. ☐

⬤ Ask and answer.

Does Rita like carrots?

Yes, she does.

Does she like oranges?

No, she doesn't.

He doesn't like milk.
Does she like milk? Yes, she does. / No, she doesn't.

Polly the porcupine's picnic

🔊 **40** **Listen and sing.**

I don't like worms
And I don't eat cheese.
I don't like carrots,
I just like peas!

She doesn't like worms
And she doesn't eat cheese.
She doesn't like carrots,
She just likes peas!

So come to the porcupine's picnic!
Polly, the Porcupine!

I don't eat chocolate
And I don't like leaves.
I don't like peanuts,
I just like peas!

She doesn't eat chocolate
And she doesn't like leaves.
She doesn't like peanuts,
She just likes peas!

So come to the porcupine's picnic!
Polly, the Porcupine!

⚪ **Choose: like or likes.**

1 Polly like (likes) picnics.

2 She like likes peas.

3 She doesn't like likes leaves.

4 I like likes peanuts.

5 Does she like likes chocolate?

Where do you live?

41 Listen, read and repeat.

Where do they live? Ask and answer.

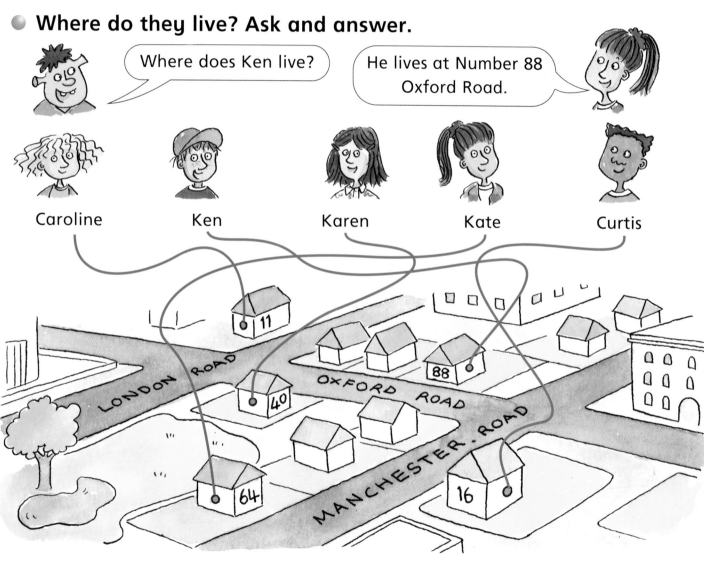

42 Listen and answer Yes or No.

I live at … She lives at …

XYZKOM POWDER

Panel 1: ... Give him a lot of lemonade, Captain – it's the only way ... Or perhaps he can stay that colour ...?

Lemonade?

Panel 2: Poor Pluto – he doesn't like lemonade.

That's tough. Tell him to drink a big bottle ... or we can't help him.

Panel 3: XYZKOM is a new powder from a secret laboratory in London. Scientists are hoping to use it against diseases in Africa and Asia, but there is a problem: XYZKOM powder turns things yellow or golden. Scientists do not understand the reason for this.

Listen, Pluto!

Panel 4: More, Pluto. Drink it all, please.

PLUTO

Panel 5: So the powder works. Now Doctor Rotter can turn animals yellow ...

Mmm. That's right.

Panel 6: But what's the **next** part of his plan?

Where's the dog?

(44) Listen and point.

(45) Who answers Kate? Listen and say the name.

Ken

Caroline

Curtis

Karen

The dog

Read and match.

1 We're making cookies …

2 I'm watching a film on TV …

3 He's listening to music …

4 We're playing cards …

5 She's washing her hands …

a We're in the living-room.

b She's in the bathroom.

c We're in the kitchen.

d I'm in the living-room.

e He's in his bedroom.

Monsters everywhere!

46 **Listen and say the rap.**

There are monsters in the kitchen,
There's a monster on the stairs.
There are monsters in the bathroom,
There's a monster in my chair!

There are monsters in the living-room,
There's a monster in a box.
There are monsters in my bedroom,
There's a monster in my socks!

Bedroom, bathroom, kitchen, stairs:
Monsters, monsters everywhere!

47 **Listen and repeat the rhyme.**

North, South, East, West

North and South,
East and West –
Home is the place
I like best.

My World My pen-friend in Canada

I've got a letter from my pen-friend, Mungo. He lives in Vancouver, on the west coast of Canada – it's a very beautiful city. Look at his photos.

● Read and match.

a I'm sending you a picture of our house. It's near English Bay, in Vancouver. My bedroom isn't very big, but I like it. Tell me about your house – where is it?

b I like swimming at English Bay in the summer. I've got a kayak, too – I like kayaking. We sometimes see seals and sea lions in the water there! Do you like water sports too?

c There's a famous aquarium in the big city park, Stanley Park. It has a great collection of fish and sea animals. I like the whales best, but I don't like the sea snakes very much.

d There's a collection of Indian totem poles in Stanley Park. Totem poles tell you the story of Native Canadian families. Totem poles are huge – look at the photo!

● Answer the questions.

1. Where is Vancouver?
2. What is the name of the big park in the city?
3. Where is Mungo's family's house?
4. What sports does Mungo like?
5. What is his favourite food?

e Vancouver's 'Chinatown' is my favourite place to eat at restaurants! Our Chinatown is great. My mum likes Chinese food – me too! Do you sometimes eat Chinese food with your family?

A rocket race

Choose one rocket. Have a race!

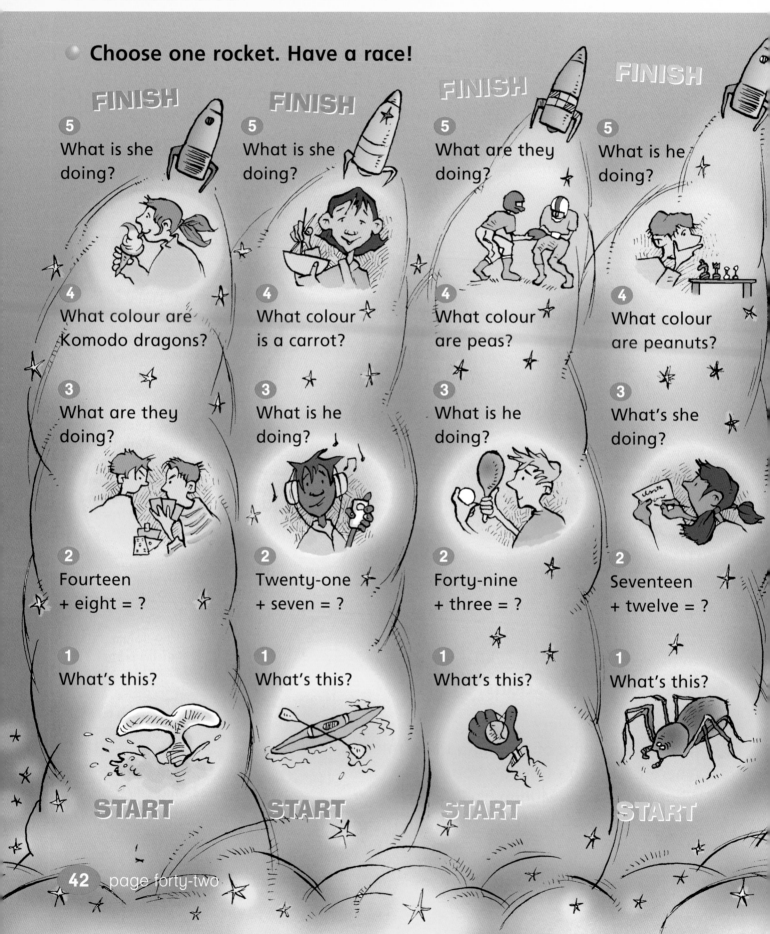

FINISH | FINISH | FINISH | FINISH

5 What is she doing?

5 What is she doing?

5 What are they doing?

5 What is he doing?

4 What colour are Komodo dragons?

4 What colour is a carrot?

4 What colour are peas?

4 What colour are peanuts?

3 What are they doing?

3 What is he doing?

3 What is he doing?

3 What's she doing?

2 Fourteen + eight = ?

2 Twenty-one + seven = ?

2 Forty-nine + three = ?

2 Seventeen + twelve = ?

1 What's this?

1 What's this?

1 What's this?

1 What's this?

START | START | START | START

At the playground

🔊 **Listen and repeat.**

I can hear **them** ...

She can't see **us** here.

Can you find **me**?

I can see **him**!

Hee! hee!

Where's Annie? I can hear **her**.

⚫ **Answer the questions.**

1 Where's Annie? Can you see her?

2 Where's Shep? Can you see him?

3 Where are Lucy and Nick?
Can you see them?

⚫ **Choose the right word.**

1 Do you like   she (her) ?

2 Let's ask   they   them .

3 I can see   him   he   now. Look!

4 Can you help   we   us , please?

5 Can you hear   me   I , now?

her, him, me, them, us

SAN FRANCISCO

Going places

Listen and repeat.

I'm with you and ...
You're with me.
Together we are going places,
Can't you see?
Look at us and ...
Look at them.
Mmm ... Mmm ...
Mmm ... Mmm ...

She's with him and ...
He's with her.
Together they are going places,
Can't you hear?
Look at us and ...
Look at them.
Mmm ... Mmm ...
Mmm ... Mmm ...

Read and match.

1. I like Shep and Herman.
2. We like Lucy.
3. I like Annie.
4. We like Nick.
5. We like Gran and Gramp.

a. We like him.
b. We like them.
c. I like them.
d. We like her.
e. I like her.

We can't find him. Ask her.

Bingo!

carrot	bed	bus	postcard
peas	tree	tomato	fish
letter	CD	insect	cooker
cheese	sofa	basketball	spider
squirrel	egg	water	chess
dictionary	butter	peanuts	lettuce

Unit 11

Late for school

(52) Listen and read.

It's seven o'clock – I'm late for school!

Cousin Daisy is lazy. She doesn't like going to school in the morning. She always gets up late.

She puts on her clothes. Then she has a quick wash in the bathroom.

She usually eats a bowl of cereal for breakfast. She never cleans her teeth after breakfast …

Then she gets on her bicycle, and she rides to school.

You're late again, Daisy!

She always arrives at school late.

● **Listen again, and point.**

● **Ask and answer:** Yes, I do. **or** No, I don't.

1 Do you get up late in the morning?
2 Do you have a shower in the morning?
3 Do you eat cereal for breakfast?
4 Do you clean your teeth after breakfast?
5 Do you ride to school on a bike?

She gets up late. Do you get up late? Yes, I do. / No, I don't.

AT SAN FRANCISCO ZOO

Kate's day – Lucy's day

● **Read.**

| Kate usually eats cereal for breakfast ... | ... but she sometimes eats bread and honey. |

| Lucy usually eats worms for breakfast ... | ... but she sometimes likes snakes. |

| Kate always reads a book after school ... | ... she never watches TV. |

| Lucy always plays basketball with her friends after school ... | ... She never remembers her homework. |

Listen. Is it Kate or Lucy?

● **What about you? Make sentences.**

1

I always get up ...   I never ...

2

I usually ...   I sometimes ...

3

... usually ...   ... sometimes ...

4

... always ...   ... never ...

always, usually, sometimes, never

This is the way …

● Read and match.

1 It's eleven o'clock in the morning.

2 It's seven o'clock in the evening.

3 It's eleven o'clock in the evening.

4 It's six o'clock in the evening.

5 It's seven o'clock in the morning.

6 It's six o'clock in the morning.

a

b

c

d

e

f

(55) Listen and sing.

This is the way we open our eyes,
Open our eyes, open our eyes,
This is the way we open our eyes,
At seven o'clock in the morning.

This is the way we clean our teeth,
Clean our teeth, clean our teeth,
This is the way we clean our teeth,
At eight o'clock in the morning.

This is the way we eat our lunch,
Eat our lunch, eat our lunch,
This is the way we eat our lunch,
At twelve o'clock in the morning.

This is the way we watch TV,
Watch TV, watch TV,
This is the way we watch TV,
At six o'clock in the evening.

Monday, Tuesday, Wednesday ...

56 **Listen and repeat.**

57 **Listen and answer: What day of the week is it?**

It's Wednesday!

Monday

Tuesday

Wednesday

Thursday

Friday

Saturday

Sunday

THE GOLDEN COCKATOO

They've got a cockatoo now – a white cockatoo – from the zoo's Research Center. Let's follow them ...

Sunday, at 11 o'clock.

They're not at their headquarters, Captain.

Monday, at 2 o'clock.

They're not in Chinatown, or in one of the hotels at North Beach ...

Tuesday, at 6 o'clock.

So where are they? Are they doing their experiment with the cockatoo?

Here, bird – have a special cookie.

Cookie? ... Cookie?

Go on – eat it!

XYZKOM

Wednesday, at 1 o'clock.

Let's go and have a ...

Look, Captain! They're in that cable-car!

Cookie? ... Cookie?

Two minutes later.

They're going to Fisherman's Wharf, Captain.

At Fisherman's Wharf.

There they are! The cockatoo is with them – and it's golden now!

FISHERMAN'S WHARF

Kate's week at school

● **Ask and answer.**

> What lessons does Kate have on Mondays?

> On Mondays she has Maths at nine o'clock …

TIMETABLE				L		
Monday	Maths	English	Art	L	History	Science
Tuesday	Swimming	Maths	Geography	U	Computer	English
Wednesday	Maths	Computer	English	N	Sport	Sport
Thursday	History	Music	Science	C	Maths	English
Friday	English	Geography	Maths	H	Art	Art

Computer

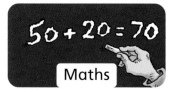

$$50 + 20 = 70$$

Maths

Science

Art

History

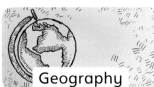

Geography

Music

Sport

● **Listen. You are in Kate's class. Answer Caroline's questions.**

● **Answer: True or False?**

1. On Mondays Kate has Maths at ten o'clock.
2. On Tuesdays Kate has Geography at eleven o'clock.
3. On Wednesdays Kate has English at nine o'clock.
4. On Thursdays Kate has Science at eleven o'clock.
5. On Fridays Kate has Art at two o'clock.

On Mondays she has Art at eleven o'clock.

Dan's Diner

● **Read.**

Dan has a busy job. He works in a café in London: 'Dan's Diner'.

He gets up at six o'clock every morning and goes to the market. He buys vegetables and fruit for the café. On Mondays and Thursdays he buys eggs, too, and on Fridays he buys fish.

He opens the café at eight o'clock and he makes 'English breakfast': bacon and eggs, sausages, tomatoes and mushrooms, with toast and tea. Dan's breakfasts are very popular!

On Mondays and Wednesdays, Dan cooks one of his special meat pies for lunch. On Tuesdays and Thursdays he makes pasta with a sauce of tomatoes and peppers – it's delicious. On Fridays he makes a special fish pie, with fish and eggs and potatoes.

Dan doesn't work on Saturdays or Sundays. He gets up late and he reads the newspaper. In the afternoons he usually goes to the playground with his daughter. She likes the swings.

● **Answer the questions.**

❶ Where does Dan work?

❷ What time does he usually get up?

❸ What does he do before he opens the café in the morning?

❹ What does he make for lunch at the café on Fridays?

❺ What does he usually do on Saturday afternoons?

🔊 **Listen and repeat.**

Desperate Dan's a funny old man.
He washes his face in a frying-pan.
He combs his hair with the leg
   of a chair:
Desperate Dan's a
   funny old man!

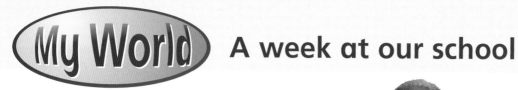

My World — A week at our school

Sharon, Tom and I go to the Park School, in south London. We've got a new friend, Adam, at school this year. He's in a different class.

● Read and match.

1 Hi, Adam. What lessons have you got this morning?

We usually have Maths and Art, but Mr Watson is taking us to the City Farm today ...

Lucky you! The City Farm is great. I like the sheep and goats best.

We're taking a picnic, to eat in the park, so I can't come to Computer Club today. Can you tell Mr Hall for me, please? I can come on Friday.

2 OK, but you usually play football on Friday afternoons ... why not this Friday?

Miss Brown wants me to be in the school play this year, so I'm not in the football team this term.

You're in the play? You're a star, Adam!

See you in the playground at break. We can play a game of tag – OK?

a

b

c

d

● Now write the name of ...

1 ... one school club at the Park School.
2 ... a popular playground game at the school.
3 ... a Friday afternoon sport at the school.
4 ... two animals at the City Farm.

The GO! STOP game

5 What is the right order?

6 When do you have English lessons at school?

4 What time do you get up on Saturdays?

7 When do you have Science lessons?

3 What lesson is this?

8 In what lesson do you learn about other countries?

2 Do you sometimes eat cheese for breakfast?

9 What do you eat in an English breakfast?

1 What's this?

10 Say this quickly: *She sells shoes and socks in Squirrel Street.*

START HERE

FINISH

Unit 13

January, February, March ...

62 **Listen and repeat.**

January   February   March   April

May   June   July   August

September   October   November   December

63 **Listen and point. Ask and answer.**

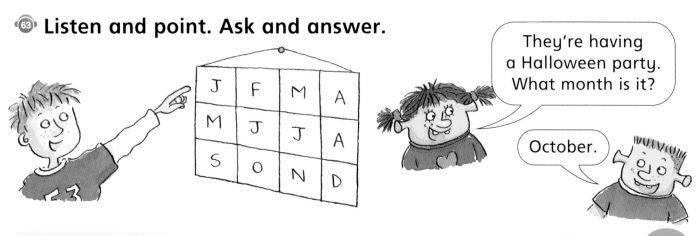

J	F	M	A
M	J	J	A
S	O	N	D

They're having a Halloween party. What month is it?

October.

ONE MILLION DOLLARS!

The first of April

65 **Listen and repeat.**

APRIL

1st first April Fool's Day!	**2**nd second	**3**rd third Kate's party - 5 o'clock	**4**th fourth Make Cake	**5**th fifth LUCY'S BIRTHDAY	**6**th sixth	**7**th seventh Visit the zoo
8th eighth	**9**th ninth No school!	**10**th tenth No school!	**11**th eleventh Easter Day	**12**th twelfth	**13**th thirteenth Visit Gran and Gramp	**14**th fourteenth
15th fifteenth	**16**th sixteenth Shep's football match	**17**th seventeenth	**18**th eighteenth	**19**th nineteenth	**20**th twentieth	**21**st twenty-first
22nd twenty-second School starts again	**23**rd twenty-third	**24**th twenty-fourth	**25**th twenty-fifth	**26**th twenty-sixth	**27**th twenty-seventh	

What's the date today?

It's the first of April. It's April Fool's Day!

66 **Listen and point at the right date.**

When is Lucy's birthday?

It's on the fifth of April.

Winter

Spring

Summer

Autumn

English seasons

67 **Listen and sing.**

January is cold and grey,
February – March, we're on the way
To leaves and flowers in April – May.
In June – July there's sun all day,
In August too, sometimes September.
Wind in October and November,
Then rain and snow, and here's December:
Christmas Days we all remember.
Then suddenly it's New Year's Day
And we're back in January!

Happy New Year!

● Read.

Is this sentence true or false?
"All people celebrate New Year on January 1st."

Answer: It's false. New Year's Day is on different days in different countries of the world.

In China, New Year's Day is usually in February. The Chinese name for their New Year's Day is 'Yuan Dan'. People stop work for three or four days. There are fireworks, delicious food, and special dances: the Lion Dance and the Dragon Dance.

In Scotland, New Year's Day is on the first of January, but the big New Year's party is on the 31st of December. 'Hogmanay' is the Scottish name for this party. Some people wear 'kilts' and they dance traditional dances to the music of 'bagpipes'. At midnight they sing a special, old Scottish song together, and they remember friends who are not with them.

People in Spain celebrate the New Year on the evening of the 31st of December, too. At midnight everyone stops and listens to the clock – BOING! ... BOING! ... BOING! ... and they eat grapes quickly: one grape for every 'BOING!' of the clock, one grape for every month of the old year. They try to eat their twelve grapes before the clock finishes and the first day of the new year starts.

● Answer the questions.

1. When is New Year's day in China?
2. What is the Chinese name for their New Year?
3. When do people in Scotland celebrate the New Year?
4. What do some Scottish people wear for the Hogmanay party?
5. What do people in Spain do at midnight on the 31st of December?

Unit 14

Yesterday and today

68 **Listen and repeat.**

This was Caroline's room yesterday …

This is Caroline's room today.

69 **Listen and point to the right picture. Then ask and answer.**

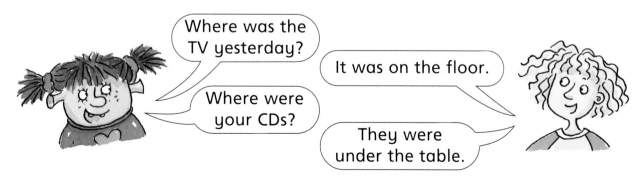

Where was the TV yesterday?

Where were your CDs?

It was on the floor.

They were under the table.

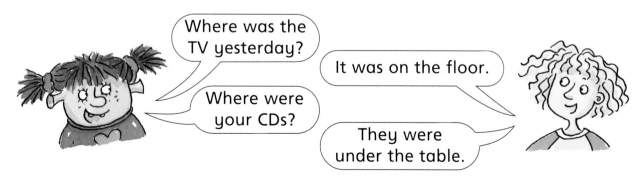

was / were

ON THE GOLDEN GATE BRIDGE

A Scottish dinosaur

● **Read.**

Millions of years ago there were dinosaurs in Europe. Now there are no dinosaurs in Europe or on Earth.

Saltopus was one of the lost dinosaurs. It was a European dinosaur, from the north of Scotland. Saltopus wasn't a very big dinosaur. It was only 60 centimetres from its nose to the end of its tail, and it was short, too – only 40 centimetres from its head to its six big toes.

These small Scottish dinosaurs had long necks and long tails. They had small heads but big mouths with dangerous teeth. They didn't have any ears or hair, but they had big golden eyes.

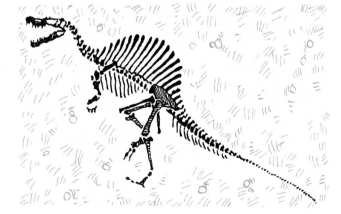

● **Answer: True or False?**

❶ Saltopus was a very big dinosaur.
❷ Saltopus was not very tall.
❸ It had a short tail.
❹ It had a big mouth and dangerous teeth.
❺ It did not have any ears or hair.

had / didn't have

Great big dinosaurs

🎵 **Listen and sing.** 🎵

Years ago there were dinosaurs,
Dinosaurs here, dinosaurs there,
Dinosaurs in trees and up in the air –
There were great big dinosaurs everywhere!
There were great big dinosaurs everywhere!

They had big, strong dinosaur legs,
They had long, fat dinosaur tails,
They had hungry dinosaur mouths and teeth,
But they all had tiny dinosaur brains!
But they all had tiny dinosaur brains!

Now there aren't any dinosaurs,
Not one dinosaur here or there,
No dinosaurs in trees or in the air –
There aren't any dinosaurs anywhere!
There aren't any dinosaurs anywhere!

⚪ **Choose the right word.**

1 There   was   were   had   dinosaurs on Earth millions of years ago.

2 Some dinosaurs   was   were   had   very long tails.

3 'Saltopus'   was   were   had   a small European dinosaur.

4 Many dinosaurs   was   were   had   no ears.

5 'Saltopus'   was   were   had   a small brain.

An e-mail from Caroline

● **Read.**

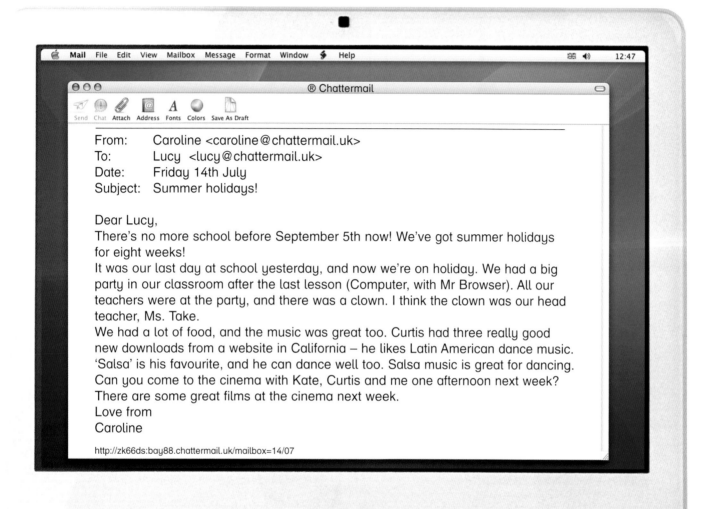

Mail   File   Edit   View   Mailbox   Message   Format   Window $ Help   12:47

® Chattermail

Send   Chat   Attach   Address   Fonts   Colors   Save As Draft

From: Caroline <caroline@chattermail.uk>
To: Lucy <lucy@chattermail.uk>
Date: Friday 14th July
Subject: Summer holidays!

Dear Lucy,
There's no more school before September 5th now! We've got summer holidays for eight weeks!
It was our last day at school yesterday, and now we're on holiday. We had a big party in our classroom after the last lesson (Computer, with Mr Browser). All our teachers were at the party, and there was a clown. I think the clown was our head teacher, Ms. Take.
We had a lot of food, and the music was great too. Curtis had three really good new downloads from a website in California – he likes Latin American dance music. 'Salsa' is his favourite, and he can dance well too. Salsa music is great for dancing.
Can you come to the cinema with Kate, Curtis and me one afternoon next week? There are some great films at the cinema next week.
Love from
Caroline

http://zk66ds:bay88.chattermail.uk/mailbox=14/07

● **Answer the questions.**

❶ What is Caroline's e-mail address?
❷ What is the date of her message?
❸ What was the date of her class's party?
❹ Who was the clown at the party?
❺ Who had some good dance music downloads for the party?

🔊 **Listen. Is it Caroline, Curtis or Lucy?**

FREE!

It's party-time!

● **Can you remember the songs and games?**

1 Crazy counting
Look at page 8 again.
Listen and say the rap.

2 The Sweet Shop Song
Look at page 12 again.
Listen and sing.

3 If you're feeling sad and blue …
Look at page 22 again.
Listen, sing and dance.

4 Look at page 28.
Play the GO!- STOP! game again.

5 I don't like the rain!
Look at page 32 again.
Listen and sing.

6 Polly the porcupine's picnic
Look at page 36 again.
Listen and sing.

7 Monsters everywhere!
Look at page 40 again.
Listen and say the rap.

8 Look at page 42.
Play the Rocket Race game again.

9 Monday, Tuesday, Wednesday …
Say the days of the week.
Look at page 51, and say them again.

10 English Seasons
Look at page 59 again.
Listen and sing.

11 Great big dinosaurs
Look at page 64 again.
Listen and sing.

Are you a good detective? (Revision)

74 **Can you remember the story?**
Listen and point, then answer the questions.

Where is this tall building? Who lives in the building?

What is the name of the big bridge in San Francisco? What is in the cage?

Where are Doctor Rotter and his sisters going?

Where are Luke and Captain Shadow? Where is Bean?

What is the cockatoo drinking? Where is the prize money for the competition?

Where are Doctor Rotter and his sisters now? What is Doctor Rotter doing?

My World — Around the English-speaking world

We're doing a class project about different countries in the English-speaking world. This is my poster for the classroom wall.

● Read and match.

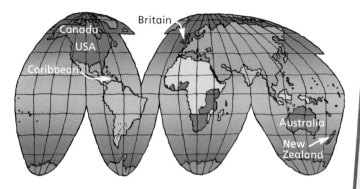

The English-speaking world

① In Britain, and in the islands of the Caribbean, people celebrate **Carnival**. The famous Notting Hill Carnival in London, for example, is at the end of August. People dance and make Caribbean music in the streets and in a big park, Hyde Park.

② On **Canada Day**, the 1st of July every year, there are red and white flags in every city and town in Canada. In Ottawa, the capital, there is a big parade. In the parade you can see the famous Royal Canadian Mounted Police (the Mounties) on their horses.

③ **ANZAC Day**, on April 25th every year, is a special day for the people of Australia and New Zealand. On that day there are parades, and people remember the First and Second World Wars of the twentieth century.

④ The 4th of July every year is a holiday in the United States: **American Independence Day**. There are huge street parties and parades in every city, with American flags on every building. In the evening, there are fireworks … and people eat millions of burgers!

The great go-kart grand prix

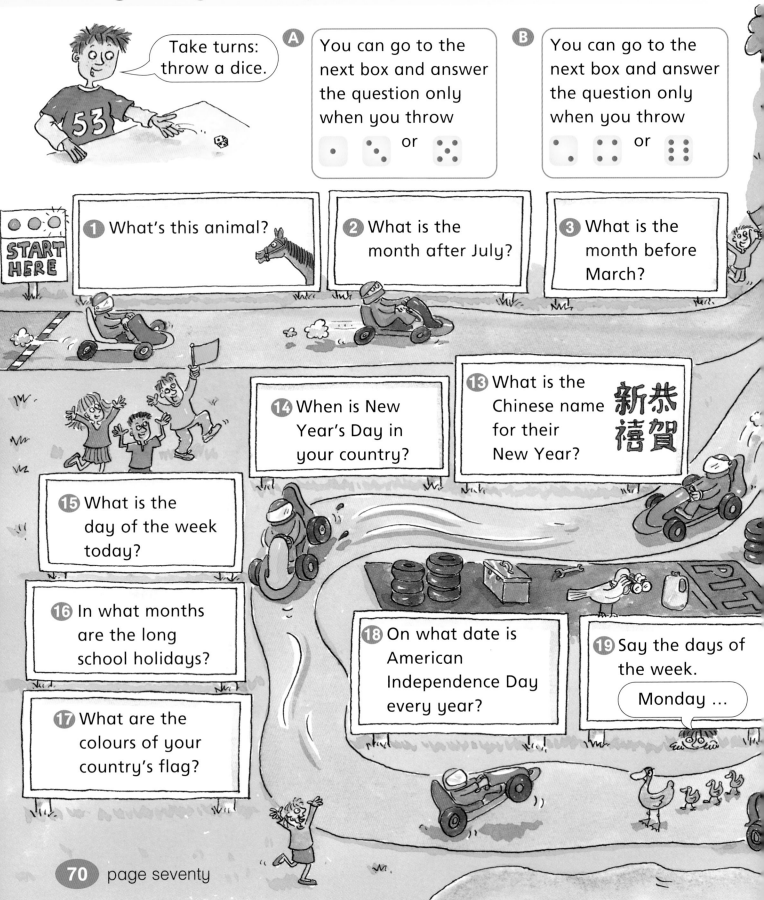

5 What's this?

6 What's this word? **T E S P R E B E M** Say the word.

7 What is the date of your birthday?

8 How many days are there in October?

9 What date is April Fool's Day in Britain?

4 How many letters are in the word CENTIMETRE ?

10 How many months are there in a year?

11 What is the name of a big white Australian parrot?

23 What did you have for breakfast this morning?

12 Have you got a brain? Where is it?

22 Where do you go to see films?

24 What is the name of a popular Latin American dance?

21 What sports do you play in summer?

25 Say this quickly:
purple porcupine …
pink porcupine …
purple porcupine …
pink porcupine …

20 What is the big country to the north of the USA?

FINISH

BONFIRE NIGHT

Bonfire Night in Britain is on November 5th.

Wow!

Look!

● Read. Find the names of four popular fireworks.

On November 5th many British families go to a Bonfire Night party. There are bonfire parties at schools and in parks and some families have a party with fireworks at home.

At a Bonfire Party, people watch the fireworks and they eat big, fat hot-dogs and burgers.

Some of the fireworks have special names: rockets, Catherine wheels, volcanoes and bangers are some of the popular fireworks in Britain. Children sometimes play with sparklers, too.

Remember: always be very careful with fireworks – they are dangerous.

At the barbecue

I'm hungry. Let's go to the barbecue.

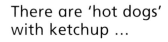
There are 'hot dogs' with ketchup ...

There are burgers with salad ...

And there are 'Toffee Apples' – apples with hot sugar all over them. What's your favourite barbecue food?

The Fireworks rap

Listen and say the rap.

Bonfires go crack-pop-sizzle!
Bangers go bang-bang-bang!
Sparklers go fizz-fizz-fizzle!
And rockets go whoosh-boom-boom!

It's Bonfire Night, it's Fireworks Night.
It's time for 'Look!' and 'Wow!'
It's time to see the fireworks go:
WHOOSH-BANG-FIZZ-BOOM-BOOM!

Make a 'Catherine wheel'.

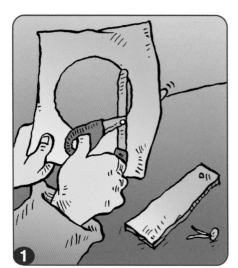

1. Cut a circle of card. Also cut a long, thin piece of card.

2. Stick pieces of paper of different colours to the circle. This is your Catherine wheel.

3. Now pin your Catherine wheel to the long, thin piece of card. Spin it round and round, fast!

● **Make English pancakes.**

Pancake Day is usually in February, but sometimes it is in March. It is always a Tuesday. I usually make English pancakes on Pancake Tuesday.

● **You need ...**

two eggs

three big spoons of flour

a cup of milk

some margarine or butter

some sugar

a lemon

● **And ...**

a small bowl

a frying-pan

a big spoon

● **Now ...**

Mix two eggs ... and three spoons of flour together in the bowl.

Mix in one cup of milk.

Put one spoon of butter in a hot frying-pan. Then put half a cup of pancake mixture into the pan.

Cover the pan thinly with the mixture. After half a minute turn the pancake. Cook it for half a minute more.

Eat it with lemon and sugar. Delicious!

The Pancake rap

Listen and repeat.

Mix a pancake,
Mix a pancake,
Cook it in a pan.

Turn a pancake,
Turn a pancake,
Catch it in the pan.

Christmas calendars

● Read.

Some families in Britain use a special Christmas calendar in December. The Christmas calendars have little windows, one window for every day of the month before Christmas Day. You open a new window of the calendar every day, and there are small pictures in the windows: maybe a picture of a Christmas tree for the 15th of December, a picture of a Christmas cracker on December 18th, a picture of Christmas presents on December 20th … and for December 24th there is usually a picture of the baby Jesus. We celebrate his birthday on Christmas Day.

Do you have special Christmas calendars in your country?

Does your family use a Christmas calendar in December?

● Make a cracker-card.

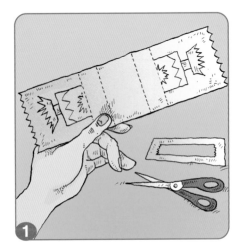
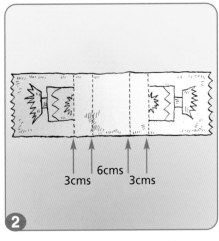

1 Draw a long cracker on a piece of card and then cut it out.

2 Fold the card in four places.

3 Draw and colour the cracker, and draw a 'BANG' in a star in the middle of the card.

Hot cross buns

⬤ **Read.**

Easter is usually in March or April every year. Some people eat a lot of chocolate at Easter – chocolate eggs, chocolate rabbits and big boxes of chocolates, and some people eat special Easter buns: Hot Cross Buns. (A bun is a small piece of sweet white bread, sometimes with fruit in it.)

You cut the bun in half, and toast it. When the bun is golden-brown, put it on a plate and butter it. Eat it when it's hot – it's a hot cross bun, remember!

Do you have special cakes, buns or sweets at Easter in your country?

An Easter song

🔘 **Listen and sing.**

Hot Cross Buns!
Hot Cross Buns!
One a penny, two a penny –
Hot Cross Buns!

If you have no daughters,
Give them to your sons!
One a penny, two a penny –
Hot Cross Buns!

79 Listen and read, then act.

Characters:	Vince	Max's Australian pen-friend
Max	Ellie	Vince's sister
Max's mum	Jake ⎫	Ellie's friends
Max's dad	Jody ⎭	
Max's friends	**Other young Australians**	

ACT 1 Max's birthday, at home in London

Narrator: It's Max's birthday. She's at home in London.

Max's friends: Happy Birthday, Max! … Happy Birthday!

Max: What's this? … Wow! A mobile! That's a really cool birthday present – thanks, Mum, and thanks, Dad.

Max's dad: It's a special new mobile, Max. You can talk to your friends in Australia and other countries.

Max: Can I send them text messages, too?

Max's mum: No problem – that's easy. … Who are you texting, Max?

Max: I'm writing to Vince and Ellie in Sydney with my new mobile number.

Max's mum: Max? Max? Where are you? … She was here a minute ago.

Max's dad: Where is she? … She had her new mobile in her hand – perhaps she's in Sydney. Ha! Ha!

Max's mum: It's not funny, Bob.

Narrator: Max is missing!

ACT 2 At Vince's house, in Sydney

Narrator: Suddenly, Max is at Vince's house, in Sydney, Australia.

Max: Hey! Where am I?

Vince: Max! What are you doing in Sydney? Are you here with your mum and dad?

Max: Vince! Hi. I … er … No. … I'm in Sydney? I was in London a minute ago …

Vince: Well, you're in Sydney now, Max. And we're having a barbecue. Are you hungry?

Max: Yes, I'm really hungry!

Vince: Good. Come and say Hi to Ellie and her friends … Ellie, Max is here!

Ellie: Max! It's great to see you again. This is my friend, Jake, and his sister, Jody.

Jake: Hi, Max. Welcome to Sydney.

Jody: Here, Max – have a burger.

Max: Oh, thanks.

Other young Australians: Hi, Max. … Pleased to meet you.

Jake: Hey, Max. That's a cool mobile. Can I look at it?

ACT 3 At Bondi Beach, in Sydney

Max :   It's a special new mobile, but I think this mobile is magic.

Jake: A magic mobile? Wow! Let's try it.

Jody: Write the words 'Bondi Beach', Jake, then press 'Send'.

Max: Wait! First, hold my hands. OK – now!

Jake: B – O – N – D - I … B – E – A – C – H … Send!

Narrator: Suddenly they are all at Bondi Beach, the most famous beach in Australia.

Young Australians: Hey! … Wow!

Jake: Your mobile **is** magic, Max!

Vince: We're at Bondi Beach – the sun is shining
            and the sea is blue!

Ellie: And I'm hot. Are you coming for a swim
            – Jake? Max? Come on!

Jake: The waves are good today, but I haven't
            got my surfboard …

Jody: The surfing at Bondi is great, Max.

Vince: Yeah, Jake is a great surfer.

Jody: He's the star surfer in our family!

ACT 4 At home again, in London

Narrator: Max is back in London.

Max's dad: Max! Where were you? You weren't in your bedroom, or the kitchen … and your
             new mobile wasn't here …

Max: No, Dad. I had my mobile with me – I was in Australia.

Max's mum: In Australia? But Max, you were only missing for 45 minutes …

Max: It's true, Mum. I was with Vince and Ellie in Sydney. I had a great time.

Max's dad: She's joking … Max, are you feeling OK?

Max: No, Dad, I'm not joking. We were at Bondi Beach,
             and we had a swim in the sea.

Max's mum: I think you're dreaming, Max.

Max: I'm not dreaming, Mum. Vince and Ellie can tell you.
             Here – use my mobile and ask them: 'Was Max with
             you in Sydney today?'

Max's dad: OK, give me the mobile. 'Was - Max - with - you -
             mmm - mmm?' What's their number?

Max: 9802 766513 … OK, Dad – now press 'Send' …

Max's mum: Bob? Where are you, Bob? But he was here …!

Max: I think he's in Australia now, Mum.

Wildlife in Britain

● **Get ready to read. Look at the title and the pictures. What is this page about?**

a plants   b animals   c films

● **Now read and choose three of the photos.**

A Welcome to Scotland! Scotland is in the north of Britain. This is a picture of a wild deer in the mountains of Scotland. A deer is a very big animal, with long, strong legs – it can run very fast.

Photo ☐

B This is a salmon. It is a large British fish. There are wild salmon in the rivers of England, Wales and Scotland, and in lakes in Ireland too.

Photo ☐

C This is a red kite. It is a large British bird. There are red kites in the mountains of Wales. Wales is in the west of Britain.

Photo ☐

● **Find the name of …**

1 … a big fish.
2 … a large wild animal.
3 … a bird.

● **Answer the questions.**

1 Where can you see deer in Britain?

2 Where is Scotland?

3 Where can you find salmon?

4 What are the names of four countries in Britain?

5 Where is Wales?

6 Where can you see red kites?

The Eden Project

- **Get ready to read. Look at the photos and guess. Which three of these words are in the information leaflet? Use a dictionary.**

  spoon　　plants　　pets　　greenhouses　　garden　　teacher

- **Now read and check your guesses.**

- **Match these questions with the three answers in the leaflet.**

  a Why are plants important to us?
  b Where is The Eden Project, and what is it?
  c What can you do at The Eden Project?

Question ☐

Answer 1: The Eden Project is a very special garden in the south-west of England. At The Eden Project there are trees and plants from Europe, Africa, Asia, Australia, and North and South America. The plants grow in two huge greenhouses.

Question ☐

Answer 2: In the greenhouses at The Eden Project there is information about all the plants. There are also competitions and quizzes about plants, and great things to do: paper-making lessons and the 'Crazy Cook Competition', for example.

Question ☐

Answer 3: Plants give us food, clothes, medicines, books and newspapers, and parts of our houses, bicycles and cars. Plants give us oxygen, too. People cannot live without oxygen in the air so we cannot live without plants.

- **Look at this 'word-map'. What is the missing 'key-word'?**

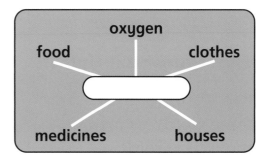

Wallace and Gromit

● **Get ready to read. The photo on this page is from a film. What sort of film is it?**

   ⓐ a history film   ⓑ a wild life film   ⓒ a cartoon film

● **Read and find the name of one Wallace and Gromit film.**

This is Wallace. He's famous in England. He's the star of some great English animated cartoon films, videos and comic books.

Gromit is Wallace's pet dog. He's the other star of the famous animated cartoon films. They live in a small town in the north of England, and they are both very funny.

Wallace likes to do the same things at the same time every day. He eats toast for breakfast every day, and he drinks tea with milk and sugar. He eats a lot of cheese for lunch and dinner – he only likes good English cheese, of course!

Wallace and Gromit do everything together. They have some amazing adventures. In one adventure film, 'A Grand Day Out', Wallace and Gromit go to the moon. The moon is made of cheese, you see, and Wallace likes cheese! Their rocket is waiting to take them home, ready for their next adventure in their next funny film.

● **Answer the questions.**

❶ Who are the stars of 'A Grand Day Out'?
❷ Where do Wallace and Gromit live?
❸ What does Wallace eat for breakfast every day?
❹ What is his other favourite food?
❺ In 'A Grand Day Out', what is the moon made of?

● **In the word-box, find ...**

❶ ... two words for food.
❷ ... three words for meals.
❸ ... three film words.

shoe	lunch	adventure
star	toast	dinner	dog
cheese	cartoon	rocket
breakfast	moon

The Ogopogo and Nessie

● **Get ready to read. Look at the pictures on this page. What are 'Nessie' and 'the Ogopogo'?**

a funny films   **b** toys   **c** water dinosaurs

● **Now read and check your answer.**

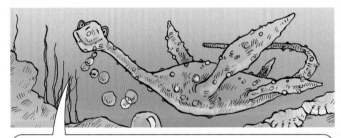

Hi! I'm the Ogopogo. I live in a deep lake in the Rocky Mountains of Canada – Lake Okanagan. I've got cousins in lakes in Russia and Sweden, my cousin Tessie lives in Lake Tahoe in California, and there's Champ in Lake Champlain, near New York. My cousin Nessie lives in Scotland.

Some people say I'm only a big fish. Other people say I'm not a real animal – I'm just a story. People come from all over the world to try to find me. Scientists use submarines and special cameras, and they think they can see something deep in Lake Okanagan, but they cannot find me!

Here I am with my long neck and tail, and my green dinosaur face. Am I real or not? What do you think?

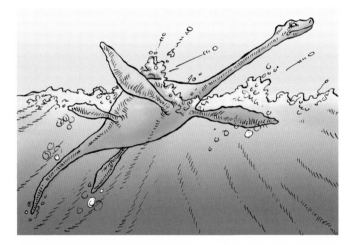

The mystery of 'Nessie'

Loch Ness is a big, deep lake in Scotland. Some people think there is a large animal in the lake, perhaps a water dinosaur. 'Nessie' is her name on TV and in the newspapers.

There are photos of the head and neck of a large grey animal in the middle of the lake – are these real photos, or are they a trick?

What is in the lake? We don't know. Nessie doesn't want to be famous. She's happy in the quiet deep water of Loch Ness.

● **Answer the questions.**

1 Where are the Rocky Mountains?
2 What do scientists use to look for the Ogopogo?
3 What is the name of the monster in Lake Tahoe, California?
4 What colour is the Loch Ness monster in photos?

London ghost mysteries

● **Get ready to read. In the box find four words for different buildings. Use a dictionary.**

> theatre   explorer   church   dress   prison   guard   museum   shadows

● **Now read and check your guesses.**

● **Match the pictures with the four ghosts in the information.**

A

The Tower of London

Today the Tower of London is a museum, but five hundred years ago it was a prison. Many famous people from British history were in prison there.

Lady Jane Grey is one example, and her ghost still appears in the Tower of London today. Five hundred years ago, Lady Jane was the Queen of England … but for only nine days. She was a prisoner in the Tower for a long time.

One cold night in February 1957, two museum guards were at work in the Tower of London. Suddenly there was a young woman near them. She had a long white dress, and long golden hair – Lady Jane Grey had long golden hair too.

B Another prisoner in the Tower for many years was Sir Walter Raleigh. He was a great English explorer, writer and scientist four hundred years ago.

It was a windy night in February 1983. One of the guards at the Tower of London was in the guardroom. Suddenly there was a noise at the door, and a tall man was there in the shadows. He had the same old-fashioned clothes as the man in a picture in the Tower of London museum – a picture of Sir Walter Raleigh!

C

Another famous ghost sometimes appears at a great London church, St Paul's Cathedral. Many people have stories about seeing him. The ghost is an old man with long grey hair, and old-fashioned clothes. He always walks slowly across the same part of the church, and he always disappears into the same part of one wall! Who was this old man? It's a mystery.

D

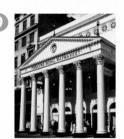

There is another ghost mystery at the Theatre Royal, a very old London theatre. This ghost is a young man in old-fashioned English clothes. He always appears at the same time of day, and he always sits in the same place in the theatre. After five minutes, he stands up, walks across the theatre, and disappears into a wall!

Why does this ghost come back again and again? And why does he always sit in that place in this famous old theatre? It's another London ghost mystery.

Choose the right answer.

1. Who was a great English explorer?
2. Who was the Queen of England for nine days?
3. Who had long golden hair?
4. Who always disappears into the wall of a famous church?
5. Who is in a picture in the Tower of London museum?
6. Who had long grey hair?
7. Who always sits in the same place for five minutes?

Lady Jane Grey

Sir Walter Raleigh

The St Paul's ghost

The Theatre Royal ghost

Write short answers.

1. Was Lady Jane Grey the Queen of England? _Yes, she was._
2. Does Lady Jane's ghost appear in the Theatre Royal?
3. Was Sir Walter Raleigh a prisoner in the Tower of London?
4. Is there a ghost in St Paul's Cathedral?
5. Does the Theatre Royal ghost wear old-fashioned clothes?

Complete the crossword with the missing words.

1. The ghost of a young woman was near two ... at the Tower one night in 1957.

2. The ghost of a young man sometimes appears in London's ... Royal.

3. Sir Walter was a great English ..., writer and scientist.

4. Lady Jane was a ... in the Tower for a long time.

5. A ... of Sir Walter Raleigh is on one wall at the Tower of London today.

6. The Tower of London is now a ...

7. There are many famous ... in London's old buildings.

OXFORD
UNIVERSITY PRESS

Great Clarendon Street, Oxford OX2 6DP

Oxford University Press is a department of the University of Oxford.
It furthers the University's objective of excellence in research, scholarship,
and education by publishing worldwide in

Oxford New York

Auckland Cape Town Dar es Salaam Hong Kong Karachi
Kuala Lumpur Madrid Melbourne Mexico City Nairobi
New Delhi Shanghai Taipei Toronto

With offices in

Argentina Austria Brazil Chile Czech Republic France Greece
Guatemala Hungary Italy Japan Poland Portugal Singapore
South Korea Switzerland Thailand Turkey Ukraine Vietnam

OXFORD and OXFORD ENGLISH are registered trade marks of
Oxford University Press in the UK and in certain other countries

ISBN: 978 0 19 472808 9

Printed in China

This book is printed on paper from certified and well-managed sources.

Schválilo MŠMT čj. 1356/2007-22 dne 13. 3. 2007 k zařazení do seznamu
učebnic pro základní vzdělávání jako součást ucelené řady učebnic pro
předmět anglický jazyk s dobou platnosti 6 let.
Recenzentkami jsou Dr. Jana Jílková, Mgr. Michaela Čaňková a Ing. Eva Píšová.

ACKNOWLEDGEMENTS

Cover illustration by: Judy Brown

Illustrations by: Judy Brown pp 1, 3, 4, 5 (top), 7, 8, 9, 11, 12, 15, 17, 18, 19, 21,
22, 23, 25, 28, 29, 31 (top), 32, 33, 35, 36, 37, 40 (top), 43, 45, 47, 49 (top), 50,
51, 53 (top), 54, 56, 57, 59, 61, 64, 67, 70, 71, 75, 78, 79. David Mostyn pp 1
(top), 2, 6, 10, 14, 16, 20, 21 (top), 24, 30, 34, 35 (top), 38, 39, 44, 48, 52, 58, 62,
66, 68. Lyn Stone pp 5, 23 (top), 26, 27, 31, 40, 42, 46, 49, 51 (top), 53, 57 (top),
59 (seasons), 63, 69, 73, 76, 77, 82, 83, 84.

*The publisher would like to thank the following for their kind permission to reproduce
photos and other copyright material:* Aardman Animations Limited p 82 (©A
Grand Day Out © NFTS 1989); Alamy Images pp 25 (Penguins/S Bloom,
Copacobana Beach/J Jangoux, Spain Festival/Imagestate, Blue Mosque/V
Koca), 26 (Switzerland/Imagestate), 27 (Scotland/Roger Pix), 33 (cockatoo/Arco
Images, Komodo dragon/Stephen Frink Collection), 41 (Totem Poles/Interfoto
Pressebildagentur, Vancouver Aquarium/Worldfoto, 60 (Bagpipes/South west
Images), 65 (Computer/P D'Alancaisez), 69 (Notting Hill/Arco Images), 72
(barbeque/Image Broker), (toffee apples/Fotoshoot), 76 (advent calendar/
Profimedia International s.r.o), 77 (hot cross buns/toodfolio), 80 (red kite/
Juniors Bildarchiv), 81 (Eden Project/Atmosphere Pic Lib), (Eden Project/Jack
Sullivan), 84 (Tower of London/Arcblue), (St Paul's/Imagestate); Apex p 81
(Eden Project Science Week/Nick Gregory); Ardea pp 33 (Snow leopard/
J Daniels, African Porcupine/Kennett W Fink), 80 (red squirrel/Geoff Trinder),
(stag/S Meyers); Bubbles p 55 (farm); Corbis pp 25 (Mexico Temple), (Mount
Fuji/RicErgenbright), 41 (English Bay/Gunter Marx Photography), (Vancouver
House/Gunter Marx Photography), 60 (Chinese Dragon/So Hing Keung), 69
(Independence Day/Ariel Skelley), (Anzac Day/Reuters), (Canadian Mounties/
Gunter Marx Photography), 72 (Bonfire/Firefly Productions), 84 (Theatre Royal/
Adam Woolfitt); Education Photos p 55 (children on stage); Getty Imges p 26
(Spain beach/T Williams); Oxford Scientific Films p 80 (salmon); OUP pp 26
(boy on bike/Punchstock), 72 (Hot Dog/Hamburger/Ingram); Topfoto p 60
(Madrid, New Year/Image Works).

Commissioned Photography by: Chris King pp 12, 13, 27, (Tom and Boat), 41, 54,
55 (Sonia), 69 (Tom), 72 (Adam), 74, 75.

With thanks to the following locations: Market Garden, 92–94 Essex Road,
Islington, London; Kelly's Café, 200 New North Road, London; Valley Road
School, Valley Road, Henley-On-Thames, Oxon; Hobbs Boat Yard, Henley-On-
Thames, Oxon.

With thanks to Robin Rippon.